# Dymchurch
## in old picture postcards

by Paul Harris

*European Library* ZALTBOMMEL/THE NETHERLANDS

GB ISBN 90 288 1124 9

© 1998 European Library – Zaltbommel/The Netherlands

# Introduction

Dymchurch has had a long history stretching back to Roman times at least. Coins and crockery have been found from this period, and the original Dymchurch Wall was said to have been Roman. A Saxon church may have been established here indicating a settlement during the Dark Ages, as it is mentioned in the Domesday Book of 1086. The present church dedicated to St. Peter and St. Paul has been developed from a Norman construction of around 1150.

The seaside village of Dymchurch was first mentioned by the name of 'Demechurch', during the reign of Edward III, when in 1374 the King sent Commissioners to assess storm damage. From the year 1252 to 1951 Romney Marsh was to varying degrees self-governing. In effect this meant government by various lords of the manor hereabouts. Co-operation between the manors was essential to ensure effective flood defences on this low-lying and vulnerable stretch of coastline. Sea and flood defence works had to be co-ordinated and paid for, so tax had to be raised locally. This local tax was known as a 'scot', those being exempted from it being said to have got off 'scot free', the origin of the term.

The governing body of the Marsh in those days was known as the 'Lords of the Level', and they met to make their decisions in the New Hall. Unfortunately in 1580 the original hall was destroyed by fire along with all historical records, so a wealth of information about the early history of Dymchurch was lost to us.

The 'Lords of the Level' still met in a New Hall which was constructed next to the church, and which today houses a very interesting local history display. Self government finally came to an end only in 1951, after the implementation of the Justices of the Peace Act of 1949 removed the 'Lords of the Level' last remaining powers.

Smuggling was ever part of Dymchurch, and Marsh life from medieval times. Then it was wool being smuggled across the Channel to Flanders. Later, during the 18th and 19th centuries, it was the more familiar tobacco and alcoholic liquor. This nefarious trade inspired Russell Thorndike to create the character of 'Dr. Syn', a fictional vicar cum smuggler who has featured in a series of seven books and subsequent films. The antics of 'Doctor Syn' alias 'The Scarecrow' are re-enacted every other year in the 'Day of Syn' celebrations in Dymchurch. Many of Thorndike's tales were penned in the Ship Inn, the 'haunted' pub opposite the church of St. Peter and St. Paul, that dates its origin back to 1452.

Thorndike was not the only well-known writer to live and work in the locality. Edith Nesbit lived in a number of properties in Dymchurch, and St. Mary's including 'Sycamore House', over the years. Best known for her 'The Railway Children', Nesbit set some scenes from her other tales in the vicinity and was well-known locally for her bohemian dress sense and lively parties, to which many famous authors of the time came, including Rudyard Kipling and H.G. Wells.

Kipling devoted a chapter of his 'Puck of Pooks Hill' to Dymchurch. In 'Dymchurch Flit' he describes the exodus of the last fairies from England in the distant past from here. Wells also describes a dramatic departure in his 'War in the Air', written in 1908. This book foresees aerial warfare some years before it became a reality. The hero of the tale, Bert Smallways, helps some passengers of an experimental airship, which has grounded, onto Dymchurch Sands, and foolishly enters the basket to retrieve their luggage. As the distressed passengers disembark the airship, relieved of its weight, shoots upwards carrying the hapless rescuer with it. A fine start to a good yarn. It was to be on these sands also, just a year or so later that Wells nearly had to take part in a duel with the father of Amber Reeves, one of Wells' many lovers.

One cannot visit Dymchurch without looking over the Martello Tower, number 24 of a string of 74 built along the south coast as a line of defence against Napoleon. The tower is run by English Heritage as an example of how such a tower would have looked in those days. After its defensive role was over, it was used by the Coastguards and the Royal Observer Corps. In fact, in 1944 Tower No. 25 had the distinction of being the place on the south coast from where the first V1 'doodlebug' was sighted. The Martello Tower chain was first planned at Dymchurch along with the idea of the Royal Military Canal following a meeting of top military dignitaries. This was held at New Hall in Dymchurch in September 1804 and chaired by the Prime Minister William Pitt the Younger.

During the 20th century the main observable change to Dymchurch has been its transformation from a quiet little seaside village to the bustling holiday resort it is today. This has been aided by the coming of the highly successful Romney, Hythe and Dymchurch Railway, said to be the smallest passenger carrying railway in the world.
The major change in the character of Dymchurch will be clearly seen from the pictures in this book, which mostly cover the period 1900-1950. The illustrations used not only emphasise the high profile side of the village history, but also that of the ordinary people of the locality. For this reason you will see examples not only of local scenes, buildings, places of historical importance, but also more intimate examples of the town's past. There are old photographs of the shops of yester-year, workshops with individuals the older generation of residents may recognise, sports teams, members of the coastguard, school pupils, the holiday camp, pubs, seabathing, days out in a charabanc and other aspects of day-to-day life in times not that long gone by.
Hopefully the local resident will find much of interest in this collection, people just about remembered, relatives, friends, grandparents from years ago; scenes not seen since childhood, and aspects of local history that may have been previously little known to many, particularly amongst the younger generation.

I have had considerable help in preparing this book and would particularly like to thank John (Jumbo) Wraight for his exceptional help in providing pictures and information from his extensive archives. In addition I am grateful to John for his further assistance in helping to sort out and select the material that has made this publication possible.
I would like also to thank all the other residents who provided information and pictures for inclusion, Channel Business Centre for the typing, and also Christine Heald, who gave what help she could in spite of having so many other calls on her time. Personally I am pleased to have been instrumental in collecting for posterity, and presenting to you, the reader, the finished work, and I hope that you will find perusing it a similarly pleasant experience.

*Paul Harris, Folkestone, May 1998*

1 Starting at the western end of the village here is a view of High Knock (High Knocke) early this century. It is said to be the highest point in Dymchurch. This is now quite developed with housing on the far bank of the drainage channel seen on the left and the A259 now running near the centre of the picture. Here we see a much more relaxed and rural view with a little sea bathing as the only obvious activity. In the far distance near the farthest telegraph pole can be seen Martello Tower No. 25, which is now in the middle of a car park. Near the bathing tent on the sea wall stand two men, a Mr. Warren on the left and his friend Billy Austin near their tents. The modern housing development that now exists at High Knocke was built from 1936 with the most recent houses being completed in 1973.

High Knock, Dymchurch.

2 Moving nearer to the main part of Dymchurch this view shows the Martello Tower No. 25 (one of 74 built around the south coast as a defence against feared invasion by Napoleon). Near the tower can be seen a line of huts used to house the army during the First World War. It was from this tower that Archie Wraight and Ernie Woodland spotted the first 'doodlebug' V1 Flying Bomb to reach England, on 14 June 1944, whilst on duty atop the tower as members of the Royal Observer Corps. Where the road enters the village proper, in the distance the houses on both sides were demolished for road widening in 1949.

Dymchurch from the Marsh

3 On the left-hand side of the road entering the village from New Romney once stood Henley's fishmongers and fish and chip shop seen here. From left to right are: William ('Wackett') Rogers, Doris Flisher and Alfred Henley. The Henley family caught and sold their own fish both on the beach and in their fishmongers. They had their own kettle nets on Dymchurch beach.

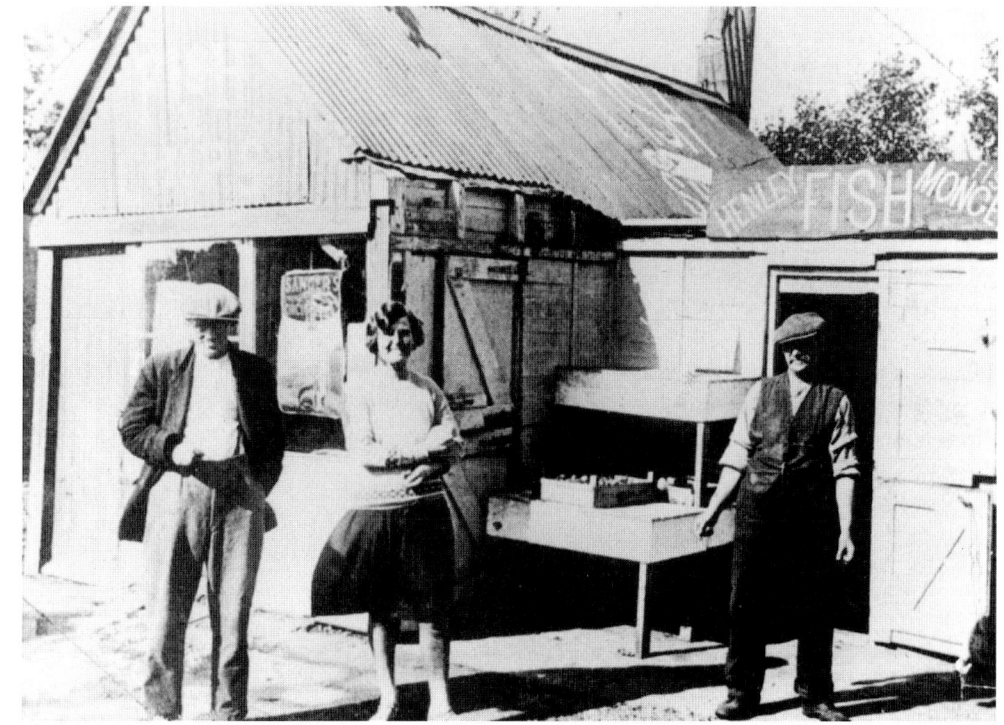

4  A very nice view of the High Street in the mid-1930's and Victoria pub, now the Ocean, but still known as the Vic by older residents. In fact, in 1949, when renovations were taking place, plaster removed revealed the pub's former name as the Ocean. It was decided to switch the pub's name back to its original. Also some rather odd things were found including piles and piles of nuts under the floorboards. It is thought these may have washed ashore from a shipwreck and been collected and stored here. Beachcombers in those days often collected everything, from tins of peaches and coffee, to coal, bottles of whisky and an abundance of timber that had come adrift from ships in pre-container days. The house opposite the Victoria was demolished in 1949 to widen the road. The village was not busy for through traffic then, so it seems, but the pub obviously has a visitor. The car park next to the Victoria has been constructed already, which along with the fact that the opposite building is still there, dates this to before 1949. In fact the postcard is dated 1936.

5 In this 'between the wars' view of the High Street the Victoria can be seen with the Swiss Cottage beyond it, one of the buildings demolished as mentioned earlier, formerly the home of the Newble family. Incidentally the original Ocean pub that preceded the Victoria dated from 1783. The pub building is probably older. Where the car is standing on the opposite side of the road is where Wellworths, toy and fancy goods store now is.

6   The grocery shop in this scene was at the time of this photograph the village post office. The postmaster, seen wearing the cap, is Mr. F.J. Francis and the lady on horseback was Miss Twyman, who is delivering the post, having just collected it from Hythe. This picture was taken on 27 January 1940, which had been the worst winter for fifty years and necessitated postal delivery being done on horseback along the sea wall since the road from Hythe was impassable, as were the lanes around Dymchurch.

7   Pope and Son, the local drapers and grocers: in fact the first grocery store in Dymchurch, later taken over by B.J. Francis and now the Wellworths toy shop. A member of the Pope family also owned a garage at Knoll View on the way towards Hythe, a site now occupied by the new garden centre.

8 This shows Mill Road in Dymchurch. The line of houses towards the middle of the picture are Wraights Cottages. The end cottage, farthest from the camera, was lived in by a Mr. Butler, who had a cycle shop on the premises. Nearest the camera on the same side is Weaver's greengrocers behind which was a house owned by the Simpson family which later became Dr. Simpson's doctor's surgery. The other side of the road has a line of houses called Mill Cottages, where a Mrs. Trice sold home-made sweets. Some locals who were young children at the time remember picking up cigarette ends and taking them to a sea captain who lived in one of the cottages as he liked to smoke them. Must have saved him a packet!

Mill Road, Dymchurch.

9 This very old view of the High Street shows (nearest the camera) the Cobblers, which is the small shop front. On the opposite side of the road next to the houses were the coastguard allotments which later became the putting green.

10  Pipers Camp, Dymchurch, one of the only family-run caravan parks in Kent, was started in the early 1930's by Bill and Ted Piper. They had a field to start with that took campers in tents only, but later installed on site caravans, many of which were made locally by Reg Wraight and Ray Smith, whose builder's yard was behind Smith's the bakers, which is now the chemist. The small caravans look rather dated now, but no doubt their occupants enjoyed themselves in the sun. Here they all seem to be posing for the picture. The Ellis family who were regular visitors to Dymchurch can be seen sitting on the left-hand side outside their caravan.

'Case carrying' became a thriving business for local children, who would take visitors' cases using home-made trucks from the bus stop in Dymchurch to the camp site over a mile away for whatever remuneration would be offered. They would book with those visitors to carry these cases back on their return journey to catch the bus home.

PIPERS CAMP, DYMCHURCH.    D/8748

11   This lovely old view of Mill Road captures the rural tranquillity of the village during the early years of this century. On the far left of the picture amongst the trees is the house known as Red Spire, which stood on the site of the Old Mill, of which more later. On the right in the foreground can be seen the Mill House where famous children's author Edith Nesbit lived for a time. Among her most famous works were 'The Railway Children', 'The Treasure Seekers' and 'Five Children and It.' Nesbit was known locally for her bohemian dress and wild parties. She eventually moved to Jesson St. Mary with her second husband Tommy Tucker. She died there in 1924 and was buried in the churchyard at St. Mary in the Marsh.

Mill Road, Dymchurch

12 A much better view of the Mill House with cows passing from Marshlands Field. Watching from the gate is long time Dymchurch resident Dot Young chatting to a friend. The cows were owned by dairyman Albert Cornes.

13  Dymchurch Station in the late 1920's. The Romney Hythe and Dymchurch Railway is said to be the world's smallest public railway service. The line opened in 1927 and was the brainchild of Henry Greenly, Capt. J.E.P. Howey and Louis Zborowski (who was tragically killed in a motor racing accident before he could see his dream realised). Dymchurch station opened in July of 1927, a year later tea rooms were opened for the use of passengers. The tea rooms did not last long though, as in 1933 they were taken over and developed into the station master's bungalow. During the Second World War the railway was taken over and operated by the War Department, but soon resumed normal service once the war was over, being officially re-opened on 21 March 1947. The service continues to be well used by visitors and locals alike to this day. To the far left of the picture can just be seen the premises of Pyrke's painters and decorators, which stands next door to the Mill House.

ROMNEY, HYTHE & DYMCHURCH RAILWAY.                                    NO. 12

14 The Marshlands Hotel on the corner of Orgaswick Avenue (then unmade and known as the Cinder Track) seen here in about 1924. The hotel has been described as being quite a 'posh' place in the days before Dymchurch became a resort. It was run by a Major McConnell and used to have its own orchestra, which would play to the 'well-to-do' diners of the time. The Coursing Club often held their dinners there and there were frequent social events including whist drives. Holiday makers and day trippers were few in those days however, only usually being seen on bank holidays.

Marshlands Hotel Dymchurch                    Nº539

15  This picture is from a postcard dated 1946 and shows Brewer's carpentry and joinery workshop next to Fairhaven and Bonnington Cottages, East Dymchurch. Brewer's were one of the first workshops in the country to make caravans, which were becoming popular just after the Second World War. They also made wooden frameworks for cars such as the Morris Traveller.

16  Inside Brewer's work-shop. Here amongst the debris of their work can be seen Thomas (Reg) Wraight (right), known by all as 'Puck' at the time, and Jeff Brewer himself (left).

17   A very clear picture of Dymchurch High Street on Armistice Day, 11 November 1918, the end of the First World War. The flags were all prepared and hoisted into position by William Henry Adams, the Chief Officer of the local coastguard. The small shop with a board outside and man and boy in the doorway, sold newspapers, and many a famous name dropped in for their morning papers over the years, including Prime Ministers Lloyd George and Winston Churchill, author H.G. Wells and more recently ex-Beatle Paul McCartney.

18  A closer view of the newsagents, J.H. Hodgson and Son. Seen here in front of the shop are Winnie Adams and Mr. Hodgson himself. Apparently they also repaired 'Wireless' sets.

19  Another view of Dymchurch High Street, this time about 1900. People all seem to be waiting for something, unless they are all posing for this picture. The wall in the right foreground on which two ladies are sitting was known as 'Tinker Tom's Wall'. 'Tinker Tom' worked on the seawall and had a marvellous garden behind his own wall containing an abundance of gooseberries, redcurrants and apples. This was tempting to local boys, who were forever getting over the wall and 'scrumping' what they could.

DYMCHURCH.-HIGH STREET.

20 All loaded up and ready to go on a Band of Hope outing, outside Smith's Stores. The Band of Hope was a religious organisation along the lines of the Salvation Army, and linked to the local Methodist Church. In June every year during the 1920's they arranged an outing for local children to Folkestone. The old charabancs set off for Folkestone with everyone singing as they passed the village pubs that they would 'shut up ol' Mackeson's houses'. Mackeson's were of course a local brewery, being situated at Hythe, and alcohol prohibition was a popular cause of the time. Upon arriving at Folkestone after a journey taking more than two hours, the children were all given a packed lunch and sent on their way. Some played around the zig-zag path and Lower Sandgate Road, whilst others went down the Old High Street and spent their few coppers in the Penny Bazaars.

21 A view of the High Street Dymchurch and what appears to be a hot afternoon sometime before the motor car became commonplace. A horse-drawn cart and someone on horseback can be seen at the end of the road. The 'Dormers' can be seen on the right-hand side of the road. One of these distinctive low-built cottages was once home to author Edith Nesbit. A local resident remembers seeing Nesbit wearing some gown-like garment standing on a chair with a bucket and a tablespoon in her hand. She was apparently using the spoon to clear the guttering.

High Street, Dymchurch.

22   Another view of a traffic-free Dymchurch High Street dated to 1909. The lady and gentleman are standing outside the Dormers. Opposite there are the coastguard allotments where the funfair now is. There is also an interesting little hut on top of the Martello Tower No. 24, no doubt for sheltering cold coastguards!

THE STREET, DYMCHURCH.

23 A lovely old picture of sheep being herded down Dymchurch High Street, in front of the Dormers. Romney Marsh sheep are famous the world over, the breed now makes up a good proportion of New Zealand's sheep stock. The importance of wool as an exportable commodity from the Marsh was first realised during the 13th century, when it was essential to the flourishing Flanders weaving industry. To overcome English government prohibition, exporting wool to Flanders from Romney Marsh became a secretive activity carried out by 'Owlers', the first recorded of Romney Marsh smugglers.

24  A very early picture of uncertain vintage, taken from the Martello Tower; see how much unbuilt-up land there is on the near side of the High Street. This is also one of the only photographs to show the mill. This was a smock and stage mill which commenced operations in 1829. It last worked about 1882 and later became a children's playground and a popular meeting place. A Mr. Davies who purchased the mill in 1905 wanted to pull the mill down, but had to seek special government permission, as it was charted as a landmark for use by passing mariners. Permission was however granted and the demolition took place in 1906. In the foreground Tinker Tom's wall can be seen as the part of an outbuilding on the far right of the picture. Rose Cottage next door was for many years the home of the artist Paul Nash.

25  Smith and Son, the village baker. Mr. Frank Smith was for many years a Sunday School teacher. He was very highly thought of locally, in fact it is said that 'one of the chief traits in his splendid character was his delight in doing good quietly and without publicity, no charitable or needy cause was ever without his support'. Standing in front of the shop is Olive Smith.

26  Another Armistice Day picture. The coastguards had the only phone in the village. When they were told about the signing of the Armistice they went to tell the local school. All the children were sent home and the village was decorated with whatever flags could be found or made. The coastguards meanwhile decorated their flagstaff and had this picture taken. Seen here are: Mr. Dawson, Chief Boatman, at the top of the steps; Mr. Chubb, Coastguard, a little down the steps; William Henry Adams, Chief Officer, to the left of him; at the bottom of the steps can just be seen Kate McCann (née Adams) holding Vera and to the right of her by the cannon Bobby Dawson, son of the Chief Boatman and Ivy Adams, wearing a white pinny.

Coast Guard Station, Dymchurch.

27 The Martello Tower coastguard station early this century. This view is interesting for the expanse of open land visible where the fun fair now is. Dymchurch had, as yet, not been discovered by the embryonic holiday trade of the time.

Coastguard St. Dymchurch 204

28 The early days of the fun fair. The seawall at this point is as yet unbuilt and a Nissan hut can be seen in the fairground. It would appear that this dates from sometime in the late 1940's, as the fairground would not have been in use during the war years. There is a roller skating rink in the foreground next to the Nissan hut which proved very popular with local children.

THE AMUSEMENT PARK, DYMCHURCH

K·1602

29　In the early days of the amusement park there was a putting green alongside with seats and an area of tables and chairs just visible nearer the road where tea could be taken. Dymchurch had then at least a little 'park', something which is today entirely lacking. This view is thought to date around 1937, when the putting green was first established.

Amusement Park & Putting Green, Dymchurch

30 The Royal Observer Corps at work atop Martello Tower No. 24, in the village. This is interesting, since it gives a rare glimpse of war-time Dymchurch. Beyond the tower, the amusement park lies empty and unused and an old East Kent bus can be seen passing a van in the High Street. The two observers are Archie Wraight (on the left) and Arthur Gearing (on the right).

31   This early 1930's view shows the Central Cycle Stores and the unmade-up dirt road leading up to the seawall. Lloyds Bank can be seen opposite, but it was not the first in the village, that honour goes to the Midland which was next door to the Cycle Stores. You can just see the letters 'BAN' of the word 'Bank' where this branch is located, almost out of sight.

32 A slightly later picture of what has now become the Central Garage and Cycle Stores. The petrol pump upon which the proprietor, Mr. Ernest (Smoker) Wraight, is leaning was the first in Dymchurch and was hand operated. Behind, at the end of the road, is the Royal British Legion hall. Ernest Wraight was born in Dymchurch in 1889. He ran this garage and cycle stores when he returned to Dymchurch after the First World War. Ernest and his wife Mildred (née Smith), developed the premises into Wraight's Stores which sold hardware, china and fancy goods. The shop was badly damaged by a bomb in 1940 but was rebuilt and continued in business for many years. The site of the shop is now a café.

33  This picture shows The Arcade between the wars. The shop was built on what had been a garden in the centre of the village in 1922. It was a walk-through shop that sold confectionary, gifts, toys, buckets and spades etc. The Arcade proved a huge success and during the early 1930's was taken over by A.J Gearing. In 1940 the shop was completely demolished by a bomb, but was rebuilt shortly after the end of the Second World War and was run by Bob and Roy Gearing with all their family helping out during the busy holiday period. There were so many visitors the staffing at times had to be increased to twelve. Both Bob and Roy retired from the shop in 1985.

34 Mullion's Paper Shop, residence of Russell Thorndike, the author of the fictional 'Dr. Syn' books about a local parson cum smuggler known as The Scarecrow. There have been two films made of Dr. Syn, the 1960's version being filmed locally. The shop is still a newsagents today. The house next door was also owned by the Thorndike's and was named 'St. Joan' by Russell's well-known actress sister Sybil.

35 Dymchurch Sands were once the venue for horse racing for local people. A minimum of three horses and riders were needed to run a race and the distance run was one mile. The races were run by a committee that based itself at the Ship Inn to where all nominations were to be made and stakes paid before 12 noon on the day of the race. Races were usually run at 2 in the afternoon after which all met for a drink at the Ship at 5 p.m., when the prizes were distributed to the winners. Although regular enough in 1850, these races had ceased to be run by the turn of the century.

# DYMCHURCH RACES.

## Friday, 21st June, 1850.

### A Sweepstakes
of one Sovereign each, with five added
FROM THE FUND.
To be run for by Horses, under 15 hands high, that have never won £10.—
Three to start, or no race.—Heats about a mile.

### A Sweepstakes of 10s. each
with two Sovereigns added from the fund.
To be run for by PONIES under 13 hands high. Three to start, or no race.
Heats about a mile.

### A HURDLE RACE
of three Sovereigns added to a Sweepstakes of 15s. each.
To be run for by Horses the property of Gentlemen residing within the limits of
**Romney, Walland and Denge Marshes.**
Three to start, or no race.—Heats, about a mile.

CONDITIONS.—All nominations to be made and stakes paid to the Committee, at the Ship inn, Dymchurch, before twelve o'clock on the day of running. All disputes to be settled by the Committee, or whom they may appoint, and their decision to be final. Racing to commence at two o'clock precisely, on the splendid sands of Dymchurch.—A GOOD ORDINARY at the SHIP inn, at five o'clock; after which the prizes will be distributed to the respective winners.

36 Dymchurch Sands in the early twentieth century. The groynes that helped keep the sands in place have now been removed, which has resulted in the erosion of some extent of the sandy beach, exposing some mud and shingle. The sands are the setting for the opening scene in H.G. Wells' novel 'The War in the Air'. Some scenes from the 1960's television series 'The Prisoner' starring Patrick McGoohan were filmed here. Some local residents vividly remember the big white balloons rolling across the sands.

Dymchurch, The Sands, No 3

37  Two members of an old Dymchurch fishing family, Pat Flisher and his father Albert, known locally as 'Ninety'. Dymchurch is notorious for everyone having a nickname. The Flisher's had their own kettle nets on Dymchurch Beach, and lived in Macketts Cottages. When he was 15 Pat ran away to sea and joined a merchant ship and travelled all around the world and joined the Royal Navy in 1935. Locally Pat is known as the 'Admiral'.

38   Below the seawall and on the beach we see a collection of bathing tents for the modest bathers of Edwardian Dymchurch. A little later during the 1920's the Daily Mail ran sandcastle building competitions on these sands. Even today the traditional sea-side entertainments flourish with donkey rides across the beach for children.

39 A 1910 view of the sea-wall and sands; note the higher level of the sands. The building at the end of the wall was John Jones' summer-house, his home Grove House is the nearest on the right in the foreground; it was destroyed by fire on 6 May 1944. Jones founded the Romney Marsh Coursing Club in 1904, having been holding private coursing meetings on the Marsh since the 1890's. The meetings became so popular that the Coursing Club was formed. Jones himself died in 1907 but the club continued.

Sea Wall & Sands, Dymchurch.

40 This picture shows a ship's lifeboat that was washed ashore near Marine Terrace; at least that's one story. Others say it was bought by Edwin Wraight. Marine Terrace was built for Jack Jones in 1893.

41  Another view of Marine Terrace in quieter days, probably a Monday (washday). This is one of the only photographs, I have seen, that shows the Old Mill. This picture must therefore date to before 1906, but after 1893.

42 An early picture of the City of London pub. Originally built in the 16th century as a coaching inn, the pub is mentioned in the 'Dr. Syn' novels as 'The Seawall Tavern'. Local legend, particularly encouraged by Sid Wood the pub landlord and Sheelah Mayhew, his niece who also lived in the pub in the late 1940's and early 1950's, tells how in the mid-1700's, during a great storm, a ship by the name of the City of London was washed clean over the seawall, such was the force of the storm-driven sea. The ship crashed into The Seawall Tavern causing severe damage and some fatalities. The pub was restored using timbers from the stranded ship, and as a commemoration of the people killed during the wreck was named after it. So The Seawall Tavern became the City of London. Among items said by some to have been recovered from the City of London wreck was a figurehead which is said to contain hiding places behind the eye balls for the secretion of jewels and precious stones when being smuggled ashore. For years the figurehead looked out from Wraight's Builders Yard but was later removed to the New Hall Museum, where it can be seen to this day.

'City of London', Dymchurch.                    N° 535.

43 This picture shows the Plater's Memorial Institute Hall built in memory of Rev. Charles Eaton Plater in 1907, a painting of whom can still be seen in the library today, which is still situated on the Seawall and is currently Dymchurch Library. It was previously used partially as a library but also for other purposes in the inter war years. During the 1930's Whist Drives, youth club activities, meetings for local clubs and 'smoking concerts' (where one could smoke) were held there. Many of these functions were for men only in those days, women being excluded, older residents of Dymchurch recall.

PLATER'S MEMORIAL, DYMCHURCH.

44   Coastguards at Dymchurch, note the spelling 'Dimchurch'. Here we see rocket apparatus being shown off. This was undoubtedly a Congreve rocket system used for firing a line to a ship in distress. The boathouse seen here was situated near the Plater Memorial Institute Hall on the seawall.

Coast-gards Dimchurch

45 The Barn House (the large building on the left) was for a long time the home of the family of James Sterndale-Bennett, son of the composer Sir William Sterndale-Bennett of the London Philharmonic Orchestra. The circular bushes in the grounds were a maze and the 'huts' nearby are actually old Metropolitan Railway carriages bought by Wraight's Builders and turned into usable accommodation. A number of these were bought and converted into dwellings during the 1920's and 1930's. Apparently young children lurking in this neighbourhood used to collect half smoked cigar butts, which one of the carriage residents had discarded, and take them home to their father's, who otherwise would not have been able to afford cigars.

46  The Wesleyan (Methodist) Church in Dymchurch as it appeared about the turn of the century. Originally the Methodists met in George Scott's house opposite the Old Rose Inn, once permission to use it as a house of worship had been obtained. That was in 1815, but soon a larger meeting hall was required and a 20 feet square building was constructed, able to hold fifty people. As the congregation grew the old chapel could not cope with increasing numbers, so in 1851 it was extended to accommodate 70. However, by 1880 this too was not large enough and a new site was looked for. The original chapel was converted into a private house and the one seen here was constructed in 1880.

WESLEYAN CHURCH DYMCHURCH

47   Another view of the Wesleyan Church that was built in 1880 on a piece of land bought for just £38 14s 0d. The new chapel was built by Messrs. Cambourn and Fox at a cost of £650. Originally brick-built the church was rendered much later in the late 1930's when a porch was added. The interior of the chapel was transformed in 1963, when a new sanctuary area was created along with a new pulpit and organ screen. New church furniture was also brought in, made by Mr. Ray Smith. Since then the church has benefitted from the addition of a new vestry, kitchen, meeting room, toilet facilities, new pews and complete refurbishment from top to bottom, especially over the last couple of years. Today a lot of good work for the Methodist Church is carried out by Terry and Ena Preston.

WESLEYAN CHURCH, DYMCHURCH.

48  A view of Woodland the grocer's shop with 'Ginger' Woodland and his wife in the doorway. School children used to drop in to buy sweets on their way home. Some of these sweets were home-made. Obviously they were spoilt for choice, one local resident remembers that as children she and her chums were always being told to 'hurry up and make up their minds' what they wanted.

49   Heading east away from Dymchurch centre we come to the area of The Grove. This picture shows G. Upton, an antique dealer. Grove Terrace can be seen on the right behind the trees. These white buildings were originally the old Coastguard Cottages known locally as Upton Cottages. They have long since been demolished and the shop more recently. The owner of the antique shop Monty Upton was a keen cricketer and captain of the Dymchurch team. If Dymchurch had won a game over the weekend Monty would be seen in his 'whites' all day Monday.

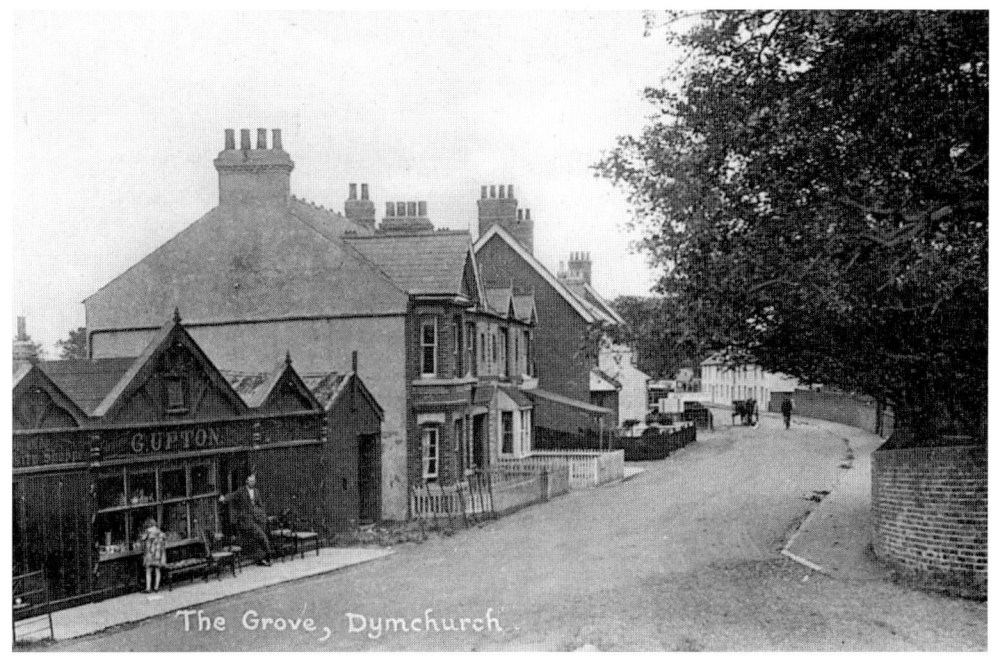

The Grove, Dymchurch.

50 This was the first taxi in Dymchurch, a 1906 Humber purchased second-hand on 9 January 1914 from Wheatley Brothers at a cost of £68 by Albert Checksfield. The vehicle is parked outside Eastbridge House in Eastbridge Road and was used to transport people to the Hythe Railway Station. Amongst the group at the doorway are: Mr. Higgins the housekeeper (in white), Mrs. Pickering (the lady in dark clothing), Mr. Pickering (the gentleman standing to the right) and Albert Checksfield (just visible behind the taxi).

51   Red House, the site of Checksfield's first garage (opposite the present one). Albert Checksfield moved in here in 1912 and set up a commercial garage in 1913, providing a full range of services to car owners including undercover garaging, washing, polishing, lubrication, puncture repairs and the sale of petrol, dispensed in 2-gallon cans. In 1924 the first petrol pump was installed at the Kerbside in front of Red House, and the first electric petrol pump in Dymchurch was installed ten years later in 1934. From 1939 Sydney and Ernest Checksfield took over the business upon their father Albert's death. They started selling cars, both new and second-hand. By 1952 the business had finally outgrown the Red House site and a new workshop and filling station were built by F. and R. Finn Bros on the opposite side of the road, the present site of Norton's garage.

52 The village water supply in 1918 consisted of a pump from which one could fill buckets of water. Obviously many found the task of collecting water tiresome, time consuming or just too strenuous, so they would pay others to collect it for them. Seen here is Harry Simpson bringing back water from the village pump at Country's Yard. He would charge 2d. a bucket, so did his competitor, an enterprising man who used a barrow to collect and transport his customers' water supplies. Dymchurch was finally linked to a mains water supply on 2 October 1926.

1192.

The Avenue.
Dymchurch

53 With its own water supply from 1926 it became possible to produce by means of hydrants and hoses a small fire fighting jet in order to quickly tackle fires, rather than wait for the arrival of horse-drawn pumps from Hythe or New Romney. Initially the newly-formed Fire Brigade's equipment consisted of a hand cart with hydrant stand pipe, hoses and buckets, which were all stored in Dick Jones' shed opposite Well Cottage, with the key at the Dymchurch Garage next door. The cart would be towed behind one of Checksfield's Taxis until enough money had been raised locally to purchase a second-hand 50 h.p. Leyland Fire Engine from Ashford Fire Brigade. This fire appliance was kept in Dymchurch Garage until October 1935 when a Fire Station was built in Orgaswick Avenue, the money being raised by public subscription. This was replaced by a new station more recently and the old building is now used as a meeting room and office by Dymchurch Parish Council. The picture shows an early line-up of members of Dymchurch Fire Brigade around their appliance. The picture is thought to date from sometime in the 1930's.

54 Another view of The Avenue, this time showing Sycamore House, the old Vicarage and another one time home of Edith Nesbit. There is a plaque on the wall commemorating her having lived here. Sycamore House is now a bed and breakfast establishment.

The Avenue, Dymchurch

55 Sycamore Gardens not long after their construction. Wraight Bros builders did most of the work on these attractive mock Tudor buildings spanning the years 1903 to 1912. The Chantry Hotel was completed in 1912. Some find these the most attractive buildings in the village.

SYCAMORE GARDENS, DYMCHURCH.

56   A scene outside the Ship Hotel, now the Ship Inn in, or just before 1908. The road is unmetalled with sheep being driven past the stables along The Avenue presumably into Dymchurch. The stables building with a Ship Hotel sign on had previously been a forge and was later used as a garage, all three uses seem quite appropriate considering the building's position in the middle of the road!

Dymchurch

Copyright. W. S. Paine, Hythe.

57 The Ship Hotel, now The Ship Inn which means it, like The Ocean, may have reverted to its original name, as a Ship Inn is recorded in a survey of the area produced in 1452. Account books of local administrators also show entries concerning payments to The Ship Inn in 1530. The earliest licence for the premises was granted in 1697. Unusually the front of the pub faces away from the main Hythe road. This is not intentional, as the road used to run in front of the pub, but was re-routed slightly in land in 1886. It was in The Ship Inn that Russell Thorndike wrote many of his stories of 'Dr. Syn', basing the characters on some of his 'cronies' in the pub and getting names from the gravestones in the churchyard opposite. The Ship Inn makes many an appearance in the 'Dr. Syn' stories and it seems that it really did have connections with smuggling in the 18th and 19th centuries, as various secret passages have been found in the walls. As one might expect with a pub of this age it has a ghost. The 'Grey Lady' is said to be heard walking the corridors upstairs at night sometimes, and one guest opening the door to see who was passing saw no one but felt a rush of air pass her.

The Ship Hotel — Dymchurch                    Edwd. J. Spicer, Proprietor

Mitchell's Series

58 The Church of St. Peter and St. Paul. The present building is of 12th century origin and has been developed from a Norman church that existed here in 1150. A church on this site was mentioned in the Domesday Book of 1086 and it is thought that a Saxon church had been here for some time before that. This church featured in Thorndike's 'Dr. Syn' books, for it was here that the parson cum smuggler preached his sermon.

The Parish Church (Of Dr. Syn Fame) Dymchurch. 1639

59 Opposite the church across Church Avenue stands New Hall pictured here. This photograph dates from about 1909 but the history of New Hall goes back much farther. From time immemorial this was where the governors of the Marsh, the Lords of the Level, held their meetings and administered justice. After the original hall burnt down, this 'new hall' was erected in 1580. It was here in September 1804 that William Pitt the Younger, together with his military advisers, hatched the plan to build the Royal Military Canal and the Martello Towers as a defence against Napoleon and his army. Right up until well into the 19th century Romney Marsh affairs, including drainage, taxation and law and order, were administered from here. The 20th century though saw the last of the powers of the Lords of the Level removed as recently as 1951. Dymchurch Gaol was situated in New Hall and had one cell that had wooden bunks for four men. Any female prisoner had to be put into a cupboard adjacent to the gaolers quarters!

Church Avenue, Dymchurch.

60   Dymchurch School in the 1940's when the headmistress was Miss Weth. Only a few years earlier lessons had been conducted in air raid shelters at the height of the war in 1942/43. The first school in the village was a wooden weatherboarded building in Mill Road opposite what is now Dr. Syn's Restaurant, purpose-built by Jeremiah Wraight. This was replaced in 1865 by the Dymchurch Church School, also known as the National School, now the Masonic Hall. Several records are still extant relating to these early years of the village school. Apparently truancy was a formidable problem then, as entries in the old school log show, for example: '21st October 1863: Rather poor attendance this morning – many boys assisting with the herring fishery? 27th October 1916: 67 present only – owing to a quantity of wood being washed ashore, boys absent picking it up. 23rd June 1916: Several of the older scholars absent probably helping to land the enormous catches of mackerel now being made by the fishermen.' In those days also pupils used to walk into school from as far away as Burmarsh and Jesson St. Mary's (now St. Mary's Bay) and there were no school dinners. The school pictured in what is now Country's Field was built in 1939; it was demolished recently to make way for new housing.

61 The Dymchurch school class of 1931 or 1932. Back row, left to right are: Miss Hampton, Phil Stewart, Roy Gearing, Daphne Thompson, Albert Austin, Peggy Thomas, George Apps, unknown. Top middle row: not known, David Wraight, Bob Godden, Dick Apps, Cyril Rodgers, Cyril Simpson, Bunny Hambrook and Cyril Wadlow. Bottom middle row is Marion Wraight third from left, next but one is Joyce Fagg. In the bottom row the last two on the right are Towser Coker and Eddie Burchall.

62 Poplar and Pantile cottages from a postcard postmarked 1912. The artist Paul Nash lived in Pantile Cottage, a converted stable, from 1923 to 1925, when he moved to Iden near Rye. In Poplar Cottage, farthest from the camera, lived William Wraight, wheelwright and 'overseer'. Both cottages were demolished for road widening.

East End, Dymchurch.

63 This shows the house known as Knoll View, so called because from it one could see distant Aldington Knoll, on the old Saxon Shore Cliff line. Aldington Knoll was once a smugglers' lookout and features in literature a number of times, being mentioned by Richard Harris Barham in 'The Leech of Folkestone' for instance. Noel Coward once had a house beneath Aldington Knoll called Goldenhurst. In fact he mentions the Knoll in his play 'Blithe Spirit'. Coward was a good friend and admirer of Edith Nesbit, that most famous of Dymchurch authors. Next to Knoll View is Corben House. Today there is the Garden Flair garden centre on the site.

64 Meadow Cottage around the turn of the century, home of The Wraight family who were one of Dymchurch's major employers being blacksmiths, undertakers, wheelwrights and of course builders. A small workshop can be seen adjoining the house. Members of the Wraight family still live in the cottage today.

65 The figurehead said by some to be from the wreck of the 'City of London', and mentioned in 'Dr. Syn Returns', in its former home at Wraight's builders yard. Young children used to be frightened of this somewhat menacing figure. Today the figurehead is to be found in the museum in the New Hall in Church Lane, Dymchurch. Local people, however, have said that the figurehead was actually washed up in St. Mary's Bay and recovered by 'Spinny' Marshall who passed it on to Edwin Wraight.

66  The workforce of Wraight's Builders in the early 1930's. From left to right back row are: Arthur Austin, Bill Newble, Arthur Newble, Jim Young, 'Raspberry' Andrews, Frank Simpson, William Tolhurst, Morris Wraight and Cecil Wraight. Second row: Hubert, 'Hoper', Bill Kennett, Alfred Austin, Waddell, Newble, Doug Wraight, Ovenden and Orly Simpson. Bottom row: Old Bill Newble, Harold Brewer, Ern Wraight, Archie Wraight, Newble, Richard Beazley, Edwin Wraight, and a young man whose name is not recorded, do you recognise him?

67   An aerial view taken in the 1930's of Pocklingtons Estate, also known as The Oval, by Surrey Flying Services of Croydon. Between the estate and the houses on the seafront can be seen extensive allotments and what appears to be very well laid out gardens behind the big house on the sea shore. The Oval has taken many years to complete, the first houses were commenced in 1909, and development carries on to this day.

EAST DYMCHURCH, SHOWING POCKLINGTON'S ESTATE, FROM THE AIR     No. 7829

68 Hythe Road, Dymchurch showing the White Gables hotel in the early 1930's, near the entrance to The Oval estate. White Gables was a beautifully furnished good quality hotel which had a cosy Olde Worlde Smugglers Bar, its own putting green and it served teas to passing motorists. Subsequent to this photograph the hotel was thatched and was very successful into the early 1970's. It then suffered a serious fire and was never rebuilt. At the end of the road on the right can be seen Slodden Farm.

Hythe Road, Dymchurch.

69  The Bungalows, interesting characterful houses, each one unique as we head out of Dymchurch along the Hythe road. Since this picture was taken in the 1920's not only have more houses appeared on the scene but more trees also. Today the scene here is considerably less bleak. The Martello Tower is No. 23 and has a wooden staircase for access that can just be made out on the roadside of the tower.

THE BUNGALOWS,
DYMCHURCH,

70  An early 1930's view of East Dymchurch a little further toward Hythe. Apart from the cars the telegraph poles also date this picture, as does the lack of vegetation noticeable on many early pictures of the Shepway area. This Martello Tower is No. 22 and the last one in Dymchurch heading east, or was! The tower was demolished for road widening in 1956 after much difficulty. High explosives had eventually to be used to bring the tower down, so sturdily was it built. Here the Martello Tower looks in good repair and apparently was a private residence before demolition.

14   EAST DYMCHURCH.

71  The Beach Holiday Camp about the same time, now renamed the New Beach Holiday Camp. Holiday camps became established during the 1930's and were particularly popular during the 1950's and still are, particularly with families who have young children. When this photograph was taken the camp consisted of chalets, now it is mostly caravans.

THE BEACH HOLIDAY CAMP, DYMCHURCH

72 The Grand Redoubt, Dymchurch, with military activity sometime prior to the 1911 postmark of the card this is taken from. Was this in connection with the Boer War which ended in 1902, the British Invasion of Tibet of 1904 or just a training exercise? The Redoubt itself was built at the same time as the Martello Towers, being part of the same defensive plan to counter Napoleon, instigated by William Pitt the Younger at Dymchurch in 1804. There is another Redoubt at Eastbourne which has been converted into a museum.

The Grand Redoubt, Dymchurch.

H.B s. F&L. No. 528.

73 A tennis party at the Old Rectory (now Sycamore House) in 1911. The families and individuals taking part were the Hunts, Cases, Smiths, Woodhams, Balfours, Elliotts, Richardsons and a Mr. Plater. Around this time tennis was definitely all the rage locally as in 1912 the Davis Cup tournament was held in nearby Folkestone. Tennis courts were at that time not only at the Rectory but also at The Ship Inn and on Dymchurch Recreation Ground, where there were two grass courts created in 1932. Today Dymchurch Tennis Club has two hard courts at the Recreation Ground, which were opened on 12 December 1992. The first tennis court known of in Dymchurch was laid by a Mr. Hunt in 1889.

74   The Dymchurch Goal Running Team, 1928. Goal Running was an old athletic sport almost exclusively played in East Kent and particularly in the Romney Marsh area. It is basically a complicated game of 'tag' between an unlimited number of runners. Dymchurch played in the Romney Marsh Goal Running League and used the Victoria as their headquarters. Locally the fields used were Marshlands, Eastbridge Road and later the recreation ground. The only equipment required was a flag, a new flag was presented to the team in 1921 by E. Piper. It was said Dymchurch had the fastest runners on the Marsh. In the 1930's the village team went for three years without defeat winning the Romney Marsh League, and were the champions of the Weald of Kent.

They also won the Sunlight Soap Cup Style and Winch Shield, Lydd Charity Shield, Bethersden Challenge Cup, Smarden Cup, Lydd Relay Cup, Ashford Cup, Upton Bros Cup, Woodchurch Cup, Dymchurch Challenge Cup and a 50 Guinea Shield, a record for any known club. There was an attempt to re-kindle interest in the sport just after the Second World War but this petered out. Seen here from left to right, are, back row: Reg Woodland, Fred Hopkins, Harry Waddel and George Ralph. Middle row: Mr. Clark (Burmarsh), Capt. A.E. Austin, Bert Uden, Jim Hoper, Ben Maskell, Percy Wood, Jumbo Coombes, Kelly Piddock, Leslie Simpson (Jugger), Brian Francis, Tom Upton, Bill Austin and William Philpott (Billy Wiggles). Front row: George Warren, George Cook, Stan Wraight, Harry Clarke, Jack Cornes, Punch Piddock, Billy Simpson, Charlie Hoper and Les Uden.

Dymchurch   Goal   Running   Team.   (1928)

75   Dymchurch Cricket Club was formed in 1888. They played on a ground in the area today occupied by Lyndhurst and Mitcham Road, and known as the athletic ground. A prominent member of the team in those early years was Richard Stokes Jones, who had played 49 matches for the Kent County side in the period 1877-1886 and was a member of the First Kent Eleven to play against the Australians in 1882. In 1928 Monty Upton, a former professional cricketer who had played in Derbyshire, became the first bowler to take a 100 wickets in a season for Dymchurch. In 1986 John 'Jumbo' Wraight became the first Dymchurch batsman to score a thousand runs in a season. Today with the club well over a hundred years old matches are played at the Recreation Ground, St. Mary's Road, Dymchurch. The photo shows a team from the early 1930's. They are, back row, left to right: Umpire (not known), Sydney Checksfield, Jim Young, Harry Divers, Albert Woodland, Georg Pain, Les Stickles, Ted Woodland and Bill Austin. Middle row: Clifford Simpson, unknown, Charles Whitehead Hoper (Captain) and Reg Wraight. At the front is David Wraight.

76   In 1947-1948 David Wraight became the first Dymchurch Football Club Captain since the club was founded in 1905 to bring a cup back to the village, when Dymchurch defeated Martin Walters 1-0 in the final of the Hythe Charity Cup. The winning team pictured here are, back row, left to right: Frank Harris, Cyril Rogers, Jim Burt, Bob Gearing, Stan Seager and George Upton. Middle row: George Gransden, Frank Cox, David Wraight (Captain), John Coates and Stan Wraight. In front is the mascot Keith Warren. In the 1956-57 season again led by David Wraight the club won its first ever league championship, winning the Folkestone and District League Division Two title by 3 points from Folkestone Invicta. Sadly due to economic recession the club folded in 1992.